Simple Methods tc

Master Happiness

Untangle Your Stress

- A guided self-help journal

Aparna Karthik

This book is a humble offering at the lotus feet of Lord Shirdi Sai.

In loving memory of my dear father.

Contents

Preface

The problem with the current world is that it is mostly filled with stress, sadness, and depression. Any person you meet has something going on in their life that they feel is way out of their power to handle. It is not just in the people we meet or know. As technology evolves and more news is shared, we are always informed of the world's happenings, which can be good and bad. Good is obvious, but why bad? Because it messes with your mind and induces fear! "What if that happens to my family?" "Oh wait—I have those exact symptoms. I need to call up my doctor!"

The more stressful people are, the more 'gurus' arise. A lot of their advice to beat stress and be happy all the time seems to be non-practical and utterly challenging to implement. How do I know? Because I tried a lot of them earnestly, with all my heart and mind. For five long years! I ended up being more miserable.

On the outside, everything was fine. I was an accomplished person at work and my personal front was great. But, inside, I knew something was simply not right. Whether it was just exhaustion from donning multiple hats for an extended period of time, aiming for perfection in everything I did, or getting hit with two cancer diagnoses within two years for my dad and sister, I could not exactly tell. I constantly felt that something was squeezing my heart right out, and I would spiral into this never-ending worry. Not just that. I was sick physically too. Many odd symptoms arose and resulted in weekly trips to the doctor's office.

The one thought that always came back to me was, *Is human life really meant to be this tough even for good people?* I figured it was not worth it. I took a sabbatical from a 15-year-long career, said no to a lucrative promotion, and decided to focus on myself. I did not know how long this break would be, but I just took it. Crazy, right? NO! It is the second best decision in my entire life (the first being the choice of my life partner).

I researched science and spirituality on the whats and whys of people's misery. I interacted with a lot of people with authority on the subject. To help my journey of self-exploration, I got trained as a life coach and in Neuro-Linguistic Programming (NLP) techniques. I started searching within for my anxious state of mind. Deep within. The deeper I went, the more I acted on my emotions and applied the techniques I learned, the better I started feeling. I found my lost self and that felt wonderful. It was not that hard. More importantly, many people may be in a bad state but cannot replicate my 'path to feeling better' for various reasons. That became my greatest inspiration to write this book.

This book is not randomly filled with positivity quotes. It does not have phrases like "You are being overly dramatic." This book/guided journal is a collection of all the techniques that helped me (and those I guided). Should you buy this book only if you are constantly worried and unhappy or your life is in chaos? I would say, "NO." Emotional fitness is like physical fitness; you need to keep up with it. But please buy this book only if you are committed to making yourself feel better.

I wrote this book to help people in any way possible with my words; it could feel like a pat on the shoulder or the tightest hug you could ever imagine. You might be at a loss for words or you might cry over and over. If it changes your life for the better, my work's purpose is fulfilled.

How to Get the Best Out of This Book

Before you delve right into the book, here are some pointers on how to get the best out of it.

This is not yet another "self-help" book. This guided self-help journal is about YOU, acknowledging what is really inside, deep inside you, and then taking action.

Through experience, I firmly believe that all the answers you seek are within you. This guided journal helps you slow down and connect with your core to get the answers you might desperately seek elsewhere.

The book is divided into three zones—**I**NTROSPECT, **C**ONNECT and **E**MPOWER; "The ICE Technique," as I call it. The best result is obtained by going through the zones sequentially after completing the exercises in each. You may come back to add more points to the previous exercise if you need to, but follow the steps outlined for every one of them.

Unless directed otherwise, read through the entire chapter once before you start recording your responses in the journal area. Follow this for every chapter in this book, in all three zones.

Spend a minimum of 15 minutes daily to attempt at least one or two questions. However, do not rush through them.

If you have bought just the ebook version, I suggest you get a notebook/diary dedicated to this book or print the exercise pages. A link to download the exercises is provided in the first chapter.

Remember—this is YOUR secret only. There will be no audience, so there is no necessity to please anyone. Be as authentic as you can while you note down your responses. At first, you may hate or even be in denial of the answers that come up. Do not try to escape from them. Once you move past that, you will be motivated to make changes that positively impact your life.

Please understand that I am NOT advocating the path I chose to get clarity in life. It is not needed as well. I did not have all the resources laid out in an easy-to-follow fashion. I had to discover them along the way from various learnings. Through this book, I have tried to create a pathway for you to tread as you begin your journey to happiness. Commitment, patience, and 15 minutes a day are the primary requisites. The plan is to get you to do more of what you like and remove unnecessary elements from your life.

Healing takes time. You did not get to your current state in one day. So cut yourself some slack. Do not expect miracles in one day. In my case, it took close to two years to get to the "blissful" state, but with every passing month, I started feeling better. There was consistent progress. I did not give up. That is what matters the most!

Do not feel frustrated or be tempted to abandon the journal if the first few exercises do not work. There is no uniform pill for happiness. Some of the techniques mentioned may not work as well for you, while others may work better. It does not matter which one works as long as there is a positive result. Stick with it and begin experiencing the miracles!

ZONE 1 - INTROSPECT

As you will know by now, this book is centered around mental wellness. There is a lot of stigma around mental health in our society. These days, it is far better, especially with many celebrities coming forward to express their challenges to increase awareness. Stigma does still exist, however. Still not convinced?

When you are in the midst of a conversation with an acquaintance, try saying, “I have been running a fever the last three days,” or “I sprained my arm.” I can bet that the other person's immediate reaction would be, “Did you visit the doctor?” Now try saying, “I am depressed and anxious all the time.” Either there will be no answer, or a more common reaction these days is, “Try being positive.” After that interaction, at least 50% of those acquaintances go to gossip about it. Why? Is it not equally important, if not more, that we are fit mentally too?

For many of us, problems arise when we suppress our emotions for a long time, although it is often not realized or understood. I have always been a straightforward person. If I do not like something or someone, it’s plastered on my face. Even for a person like me, there are many instances where I could not speak my mind freely or react to situations the way I wanted to, for various reasons. I thought I was ignoring them; little did I know I had locked up a lot of those emotions unknowingly for years. I was way too busy, professionally and personally, to take care of my emotional needs.

Life was all good and happy. Or so I thought.

As years went by, I started to realize that I was no longer able to connect with my true self. With no proper nurturing, my body and mind got tired and started giving up. When I realized that they gave me an ultimatum, I finally caved in and started acting on it; that led me to the path of healing. I understood it late, but as they say, "Better late than never."

You may have bottled up emotions unknowingly like me, or you may be a person who generally has difficulty in expressing your feelings. If your inner self is being masked, it starts turning into rage, exhaustion, and disappointment over time. It is not good for your mental health to hoard up emotions.

Did you know that emotional constipation can lead to a plethora of physical diseases as well? Every emotion you have is associated with neuropeptides. Not to turn too scientific—simply put, there are many chemicals within your body that connect it with your mind. Prolonged negativity will make you more susceptible to physical illness.

Do not let your emotions stagnate. Be in control. Find a safe outlet. Do not fear judgment. Let them flow!

The "INTROSPECT" zone will help you with this. This zone is probably the most important of all, and only you have all the answers to it. So take your time to think through and express your state.

In this section, you will interact with your true self. We will capture YOU as a whole—the past/present and then determine how you want to shape your future. Take as much time as you need to complete the exercises; please do not rush through them. No one can fix the time for contemplation—if you need four days to finish each exercise, take them.

At the end of it all, we will get your body and mind working together in a balanced way, leading to a HEALTHIER YOU!

I1: Me, Myself

We will start by recording your current state of mind. It will help evaluate your progress as you travel further.

Start the exercise when you are comfortable and reflect upon yourself without the pressure of any impending tasks. While doing this exercise, do not express how you feel that minute or even that day. It should be a cumulative feeling of a significant period, say the last week or month. Do not go into specifics of why you feel this way; just capture how you feel.

Try to finish this exercise in one go, so you have a dated record of your feelings. However, if your emotions get ramped up and you need to cool off a bit, please do not hesitate. Do not force-write. Just make sure you date the sections accordingly.

If you would like to get a soft copy of the exercises in this journal to print and follow-along, please head to: http://rakwrites.com/the-resources. Password is provided in the last chapter.

Wishing you all the very best as you start this journey of self-discovery, healing, and attracting happiness.

ME, MYSELF

INTROSPECTION NO 1 DATE:

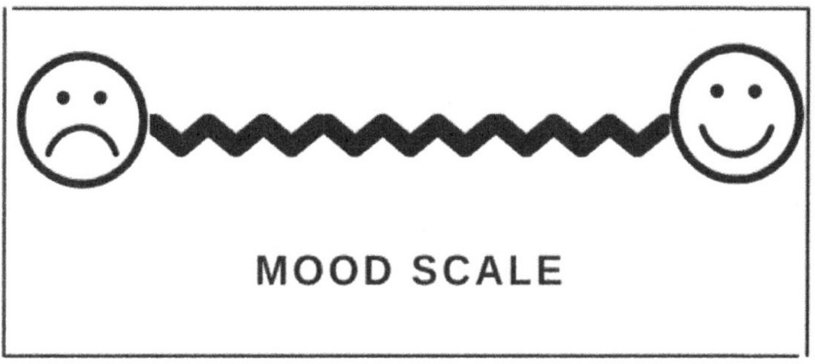

Add just a little note to record how you feel.

12: Magic Pizza, Anyone?

Before we start, here is a heads-up: This task is the longest in the entire book and will involve a lot of pondering. You may feel overwhelmed if you try to attempt all the questions in one go. You may break them up into a few mini-sessions as you like.

Why does the title say "Magic Pizza?" What are the steps to make it?

You are going to take a snapshot of all the significant areas in your life and build this magic pizza. This pizza is going to represent your current life as a whole. There may be various areas in your life, and you may be performing multiple roles in each area. Think of the pizza slice as your area and the toppings as your roles. You may like some, you may hate some, but you do it nevertheless because you are forced to. Bring them all out.

Below is an example of a magic pizza. Each slice represents a major area/part of one's life. Do not be focused on having eight slices. You may cut it into however many pieces you want. As general guidance, have six to 10.

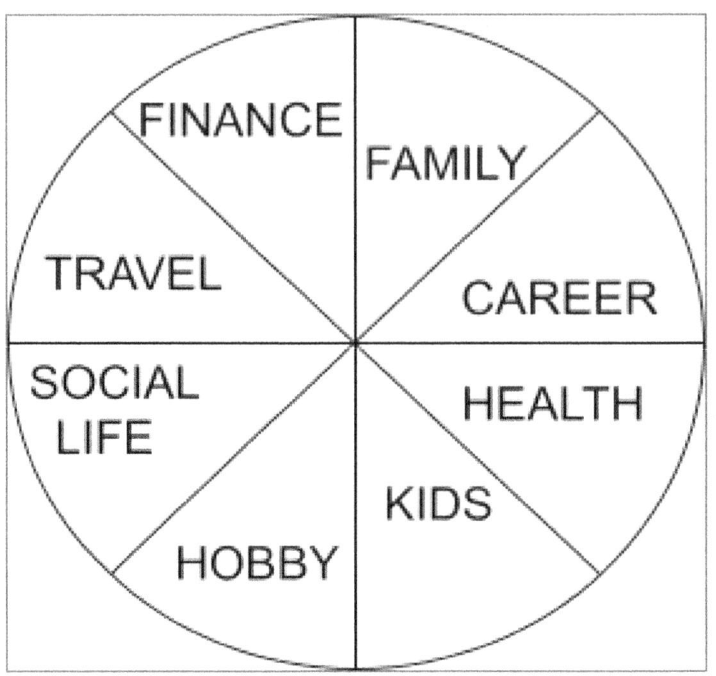

Draw your pizza here -

Now that you have cleverly identified the critical pieces that make your life meaningful, identify the roles you play in each/responsibilities you need to shoulder. You may also list things you would like to do in each area but are not doing for various reasons. Your ultimate goal is to improve the score in each area by doing more of what you like and what helps you grow as an individual.

As an example,

Area: Career
Roles: Working as a consultant, present sales pitches to potential customers, continuous self-learning/enablement, mentor team members, work towards the next role, look for a job change...

Once you have identified the areas and roles, think about how you perform in each area as a whole. Then, on a scale of 1 to 10, 1 being the least and 10 the most, start grading yourself—no grace marks. There is no pass or fail. The goal is to fare better in time to come.

You can create a template as below in the journal area or document the roles by the side of the pizza slices. Whatever works for you!

SAMPLE TEMPLATE:

AREA	ROLES	SCORE
FINANCE		
FAMILY		
CAREER		
HEALTH		
KIDS		
HOBBY		
SOCIAL LIFE		
TRAVEL		

Wait, I almost missed telling you why I call it the "Magic Pizza." This pizza weaves its magic to draw YOUR attention to YOU and instills awareness. Remember, the first steps to excellence are to identify and acknowledge.

MAGIC PIZZA

INTROSPECTION NO 2A DATE:

List your areas, roles and score. Use the table format given above or any template you like.

Pick an area that you have scored the least. Is the score the highest you have ever been in that area?

If not, what did you do before that you are not doing now?

What do you have to do to get to that score?
List some possible action points.

Pick another area that you have scored the least. Is the score the highest you have ever been in that area?

If not, what did you do before that you are not doing now?

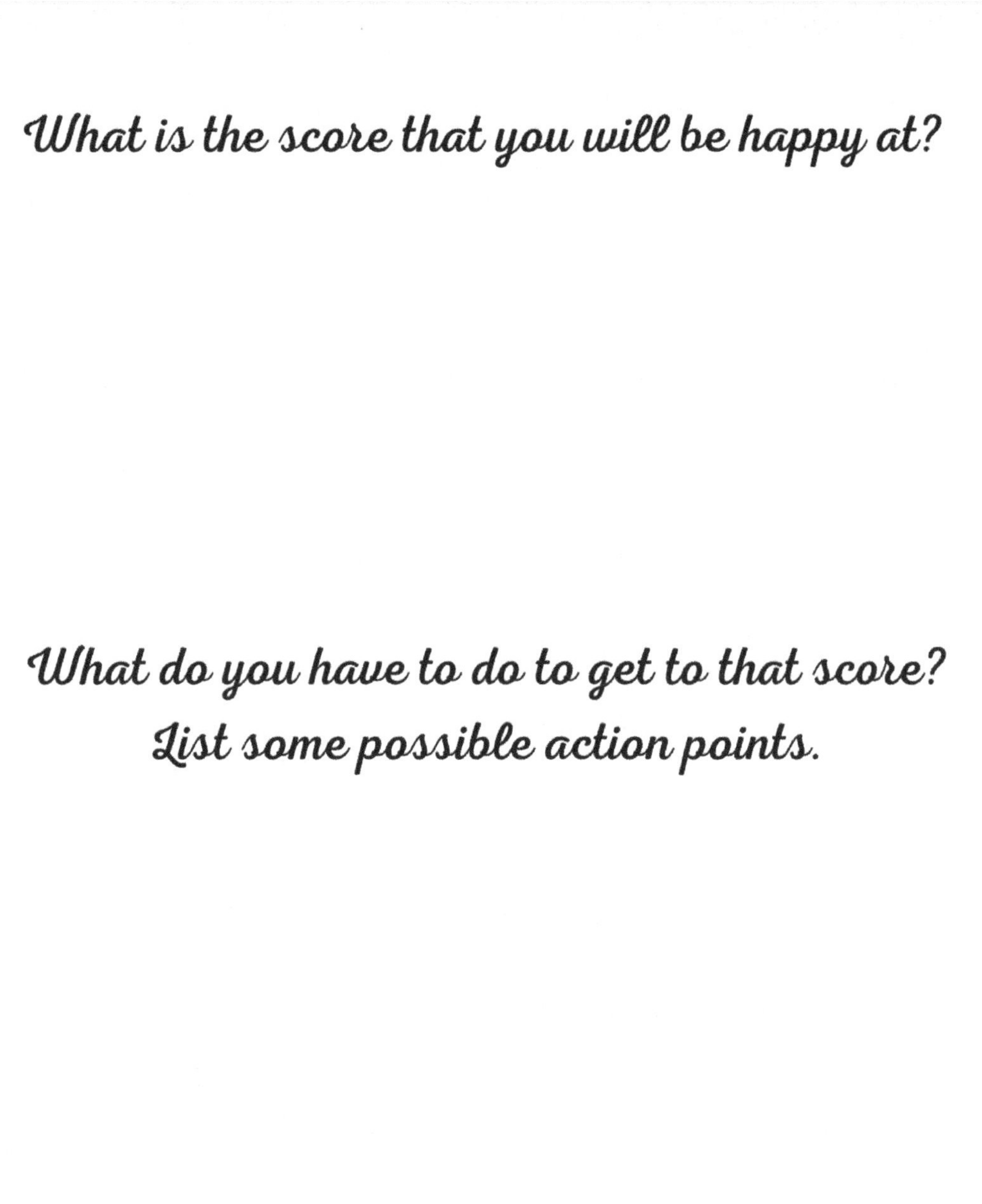

What is the score that you will be happy at?

What do you have to do to get to that score?
List some possible action points.

Follow this exercise for any other area in your life.

Anything else you would like to record?

INTROSPECTION NO 2B DATE:

Now start looking closely at the roles you have listed in each area.

Do any of them give you pleasure?

If yes, are you consistent in doing them?

If you do them more, will your score improve?

If yes, what prevents you from doing more of what you like?

Do you hate doing any of these things?

If they are not fruitful and you eliminate them, does your score improve?

What is preventing you from eliminating them?

Can they be outsourced?

Do you have points to work on in the above sections? Just note them down here. You do not have to act on them immediately.

13: I Choose 'ME'!

The last exercise included a lot of introspection. Today, you are not going to think deeply. Today, you are just going to choose yourself over everyone else because what you feel about yourself matters the most.

If you think you are a good cook and want to make lasagna from scratch for dinner, just do it. Your kids may not like your cooking. That does not count. Don't focus on the opinion of others; just focus on YOURS.

If you have locked up the sewing machine your mother gifted in the attic just because your husband thinks you are not patient enough to sew (but you secretly want to learn sewing), look up the sewing classes that fit your schedule and enroll.

Have too many ideas? Record them first.

Not in the right frame of mind to do something just for yourself yet? No problem. Record them now anyway; you will be prompted to do them in the later exercises.

Just one thing... Do it because YOU want to.

Recognize your worth. You do not need to prove a point to anyone.

Leave out the impressions created by others. You cannot please everyone.

It is high time you started doing things you wanted to do!

Ready?

I CHOOSE ME!

INTROSPECTION NO 3 DATE:

Note down 10 positive things that you really like about you - they can be skills or qualities.

Note down ten things that you want to do or like to do.

Keep in mind -

- It does not have to be something you have tried before
- It does not have to be something you are good at
- It should not involve doing something for someone else—just for YOURSELF

Like, "Take a day off from work and binge-watch your favorite movies/TV series."

Homework:

Before the next exercise, pick one thing.

And just do it!

Ongoing Homework:

Do them all!

14: Roleplay

The human mind is bizarre. When you are facing adversity, it freezes and brings only negative thought patterns. However, if the same problem is met by a friend or family member, it will give creative resolutions. Have you ever felt that way?

My friends and colleagues often come to me seeking my guidance in some aspect. They say my suggestions help them solve their problems without much hassle as I give solutions with a creative spin.

If I was so resourceful, why was I not able to help myself? I did not even realize something was off for a very long time! Every passing day added more reasons for me to be anxious about. If I were to think now, some of them were very stupid. If any of my friends were stressed for the same reasons, my response would have been, "Are you out of your mind?" But I did not play by the same rules. They were valid concerns for me. I had solid counter-arguments for every solution given by those close to me.

I was not like this before. Some settings got changed in between and I was emitting the wrong frequency signals. I could not point to a single reason for this change—just a cumulative effect of life happenings. But it did not feel good. Something was always choking me and I wanted things to be back to how they were before.

My primary care doctor suggested I try this technique and it started working, slowly but steadily. Over the years, I have fine-tuned it to my needs, but it works like a charm every time.

Curious?

ROLE PLAY

INTROSPECTION NO 4 DATE:

If you had to pick one thing that you are always stressed or anxious or worried about, what would it be?

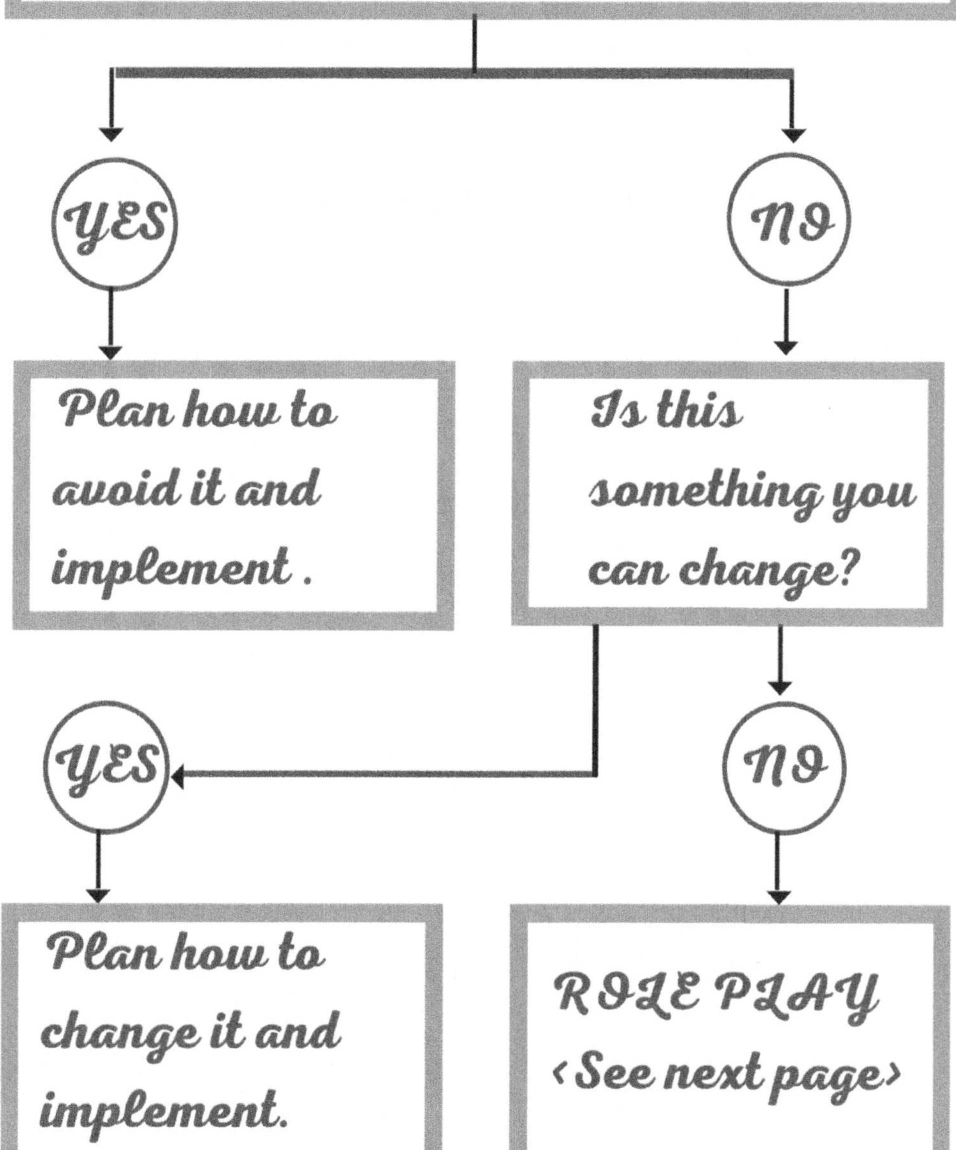
Is this something you can avoid?
YES
NO
Plan how to avoid it and implement .
Is this something you can change?
YES
NO
Plan how to change it and implement.
ROLE PLAY
‹See next page›

If you answered 'NO' and 'NO' in the flow-chart, let us do a role play.

Imagine you do not have this worry, but your close friend from school has it. Your friend has reached out to you for guidance.

What would you suggest?

Use the suggestions as is / adapt to your needs.

15: That's the Goal!

What are goals? Why are they necessary? How can you make them happen?

Many of us choose an auspicious day, say our birthday or New Year's, and list some goals/resolutions for the year. But, how many of us have even followed them up to see if we have achieved them? We mostly don't—because we know the answer! There would have been a minimal accomplishment. We might have a plethora of excuses, some reasonable, some not so much. But are we not capable of rising beyond the excuses?

Let us try something different that will help you stick with your goal and achieve it—because you deserve it!

Here is the detailed magic process. You can read them through first and then record your answers in the journal area.

1. Choose only one goal—one that is very important to you, one that will positively affect your life, one that you will be proudly able to shout from the rooftop of your building when achieved, and the one that you have been putting off for a long time. You can also choose one from the list you have from Introspection 2.

2. Write it down on paper—in BOLD. And stick it in a place where you will see it frequently. That is standard advice, right? Let us add more to this.

3. Choose a date by which you want to achieve it and write it down on the same paper. It should be a realistic date. Do not be hard on yourself.

4. What are short milestones in achieving that goal? Write them down in this journal. Date them. Set some self-calendar reminders to check if you have completed them. You will have!

5. What are the risks in achieving that goal? How can they be mitigated? Write them down. And label the section as "Action Plan."

6. Now the most important step: Think of a dear family member/friend/any well-wisher who will be the happiest when you have accomplished that goal. It can be one person, or it can be four. That is your choice. But definitely at least one who you can meet when the goal is achieved. And ... just block their time. Say that you will be coming down to give them a surprise! Don't say anything more—not now, not until the goal is achieved! And start working towards the goal!

There! You have a process. You now clearly know what you want to achieve, the action points, the risks, the milestones, the date by which you will have achieved it, and you have arranged the celebration too! Use the following few pages to pen down the plan of action.

You can follow the same process for all those items listed in Introspection 2, surprising different people in your life.

THAT'S THE GOAL!

INTROSPECTION NO 5 DATE:

What is THE GOAL you will accomplish?

By when will you accomplish this?

Set self-calendar invites for these dates

Action Plan

Risks in achieving the goal and mitigations

Whom are you planning to surprise with this achievement? Block their time .

Where will the celebration be?

Do not forget to take care of the necessary arrangements - book venue, tickets, etc.

16: Speak Your Mind!

Have you observed young kids freely speaking their minds? They have no reservations; they are not afraid of being called "crazy" or "stupid"; they do not worry about repercussions. They just speak their mind. Unfortunately, somewhere between being that kid and being the adult we are now, many of us have started holding our thoughts. But why? Everyone is entitled to their thoughts and opinions.

Speaking your mind does not mean you have to argue or sound rude. It just means that you need to express yourself truly. It will make you feel very powerful and give you a lot of satisfaction.

Do not fear, as there is no right or wrong, just opinions and beliefs. No one knows everything. Take your stand!

This task is my favorite and has helped me a lot. I still use it at times when I am reminded of any past occurrences or have a "must-hold-my-tongue" moment.

In this exercise, we will use the freewriting technique to get you to speak your mind.

Haven't you started already?

SPEAK YOUR MIND!

INTROSPECTION NO 6 DATE:

Have you previously held your tongue about your nagging spouse, your opportunistic friend, or an unethical colleague? Empty it all out.

Here is your prompt - "How I wish I'd told you this!"

17: Pyramid of Worry

Do you worry a lot? Are you always concerned that something bad will happen with your job, relationship, health, kids, and everything you are even just remotely connected to?

A wise man once said, "Worrying does not take away tomorrow's troubles. It takes away today's peace." Unfortunately, worry is part and parcel of our life these days. It would be nearly impossible for anyone to honestly say, "I do not worry about anything any day." However, chronic, incessant worrying is a problem.

Have you noticed that most of our worries never come true? That's because worry is just an emotion created by the mind, based on the thoughts you are feeding it. It is only your perspective that something could go wrong. It may or may not.

Today, you will build a pyramid of your worries. Go deep and bring out all the big and small worries your mind currently houses. It could be about you, someone you care about, some situation at work, anything.

Have more worries than one pyramid could hold? Not a problem. Do not neglect them. Draw additional pyramids. Let them all out. Label them.

I usually use the tip of the pyramid for a more time-sensitive worry, like something that might happen in the next day or two, and the bottom for something that may occur after a substantial time, say a year. Once you feel a vast majority have been recorded, you will start analyzing them.

Beginning with the tip of the pyramid, examine if there is anything you can do to impact the outcome of the worry and to what extent. Then, start labeling them as FAW/PAW/NAW.

FAW - Fully **A**ctionable **W**orry. YOU can control the outcome of the worry with some action on your part. So just list what you need to do and drop the worry.

PAW - Part **A**ctionable **W**orry. You can do your best to have the desired outcome, but it is not entirely in your hands. List your action and just do it. Drop the worry, as you know what part to play, and hope for the best.

NAW - Non-**A**ctionable **W**orry. You cannot control the outcome even if you try your best. It is entirely someone else's decision.

How can you worry about something that you cannot control? Just drop the worry.

To give an example for each type,
Worry: I am worried that I may be late for my interview tomorrow.
Classification: Fully Actionable Worry or **FAW**.
Action: Set the alarm for 30 to 45 minutes before you planned to. Start an hour early to the interview so that you can avoid last-minute delays or tension.

Worry: I am worried that my manager will promote someone else instead of me.
Classification: Part Actionable Worry or **PAW**.
Action: Have a proactive discussion with your manager about your intentions and expectations. Highlight your contributions to the team to explain how you make the best candidate for the role.

Worry: I am worried if Susan will like me the same way I like her.
Classification: Non-Actionable Worry or **NAW**.
Action: No need to record anything. Just be your true self around her.

Now it is your turn. Classify each of your worries as FAW/PAW/NAW. Record the action only if it is a FAW/PAW.

There—you have it! All the biggest and smallest of your worries and your action points, if any. Stop worrying now because YOU have it under control!

PYRAMID OF WORRY

INTROSPECTION NO 7 DATE:

List your worries and build your pyramid. Also, classify them as FAW, PAW or NAW

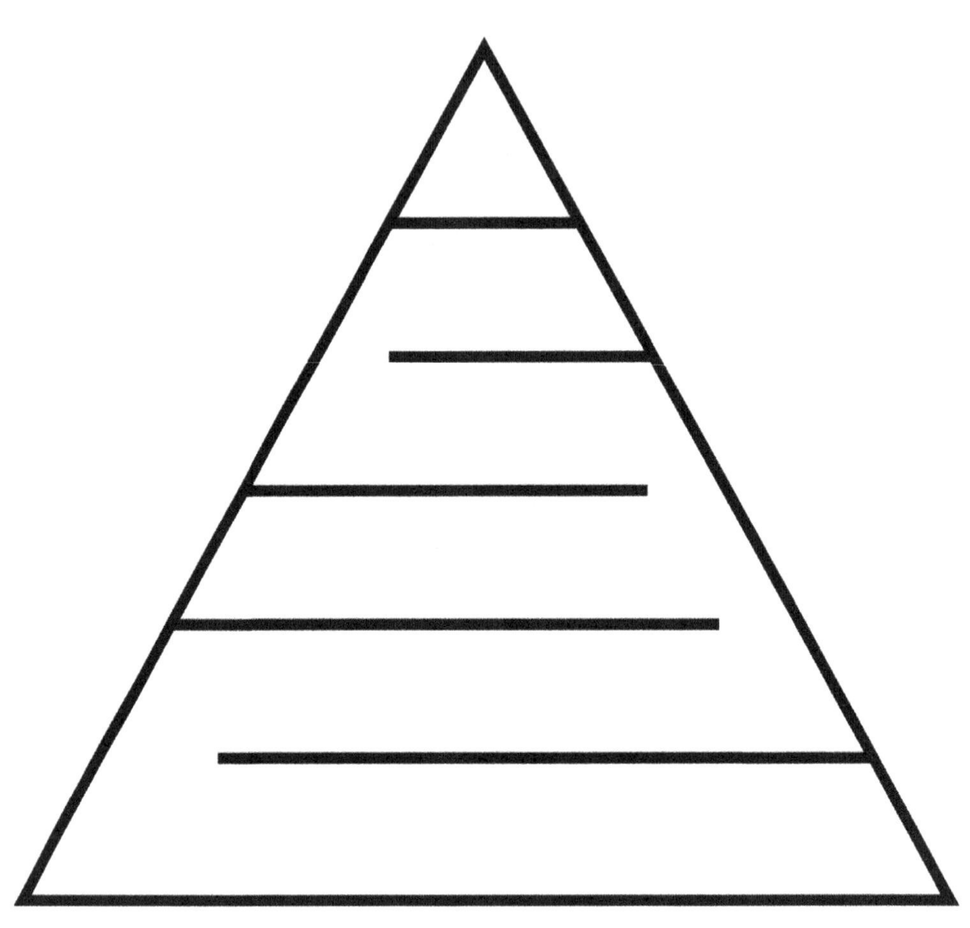

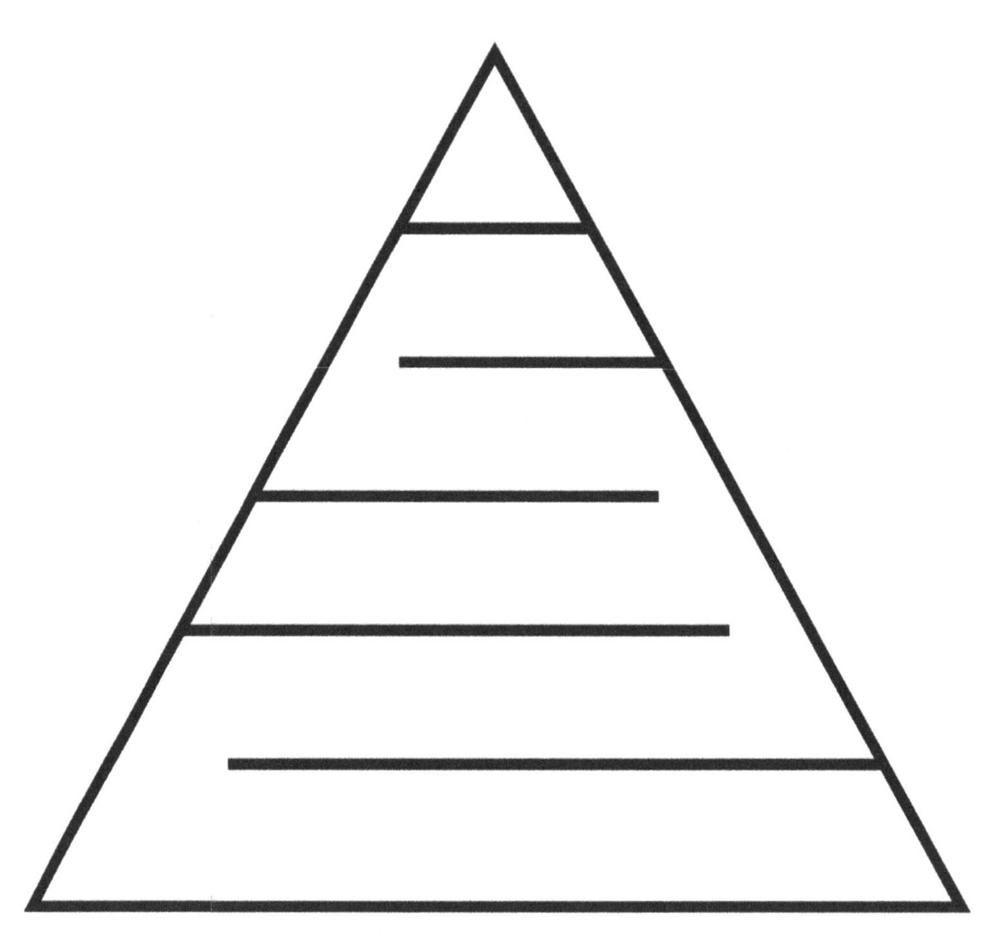

18: True or False?

Are you someone who uses a lot of negative self-talk? Where is it coming from?

Your mind!

Over the years, you have listened to a lot of criticism from parents, friends, siblings, colleagues, managers, spouses, kids, neighbors, and sometimes even yourself. It has accumulated, accentuated, and amplified but occasionally proven right. However, your mind has gotten you convinced that it is the absolute truth. In this fast-paced world, you do not even have the time to think whether it is accurate or just someone's perception. You have the time now!

Now, in the next section, list down <u>ten</u> things that you think about yourself.

Not your mom's. Not your spouse's. <u>Your</u> perception alone.

Come back to this section after you have made your entries in the journal area.

Your answers could be along the lines of "No one likes me" or "I am a great dancer." The former is a negative attribute, and the latter is a positive attribute.

If all the ten entries you listed are positive attributes, you can skip this exercise. Great job!

If you have even one negative attribute, continue to read on.

For every negative attribute you have listed, list four facts that make you think that way. Again—only facts/observations, not others' opinions/assumptions.

In the same example as above, facts can be similar to those below:
Attribute - No one likes me.
Facts - 1. I do not get invited to any parties 2. No one at my work wants to be friends with me 3. No one in my family has spoken to me in over four years 4. I do not have anyone I can call for help.

Now it is your turn. Start entering the facts that complement the negative attributes recorded.

Are you struggling to get the facts out? Or are they spewing?

Once we sit down and try to get the facts out, most of the time, we do not get many to list because we have been force-fed perspectives and made to believe them. Start ignoring the thoughts that you do not resonate with. Fill them with more positive ones. Once you start doing that, you will start getting more confident.

It does not matter what my fourth-grade art teacher thought of me. I am great at art, and I do it because it calms my mind. I do it because I like it. Period.

TRUE OR FALSE?

INTROSPECTION NO 8 DATE:

What do YOU really think about YOU?

Negative Attributes / Facts

19: Face Your Triggers

Is anxiety wreaking havoc on your body? Worried if someone/something will bring back the memories of an event/person that you have pocketed deep down and labeled "Danger! Do not open"?

Well, what are they? How long do you want to keep running away from them?

Stress, anxiety, and worry can change many things inside your body in a bad way. When you perceive danger, the frontal lobes in your brain process the situation while determining the best logical response. It works hand in hand with the amygdala, a small part in your brain that activates your fight-or-flight response for severe threats.

As stress constantly accumulates and turns into fear, the amygdala starts overpowering the frontal lobes, automatically activates the fight-or-flight response, and makes you react irrationally even for less severe threats. That is not good.

The goal is to reduce this amygdala hyperactivity and make your frontal lobes regain their power. One of the many ways to achieve this is to identify the stressors, prepare for situations that might cause this override, and constantly train your brain.

Use the template below for all of your “triggers” of fear. Let them out in the open. Prepare. Assure your mind that you will rise above the situation because you are a warrior who is prepared. And you will be unperturbed when that happens.

FACE YOUR TRIGGERS

INTROSPECTION NO 9 DATE:

What memory are you fighting so hard to forget? Why?

What are known triggers that will get you reminded of it?

Can these triggers be avoided (even if it means you might have to hurt someone's feelings)?

If any of them cannot be avoided, list them down.

When you face the trigger, what is the worst-case scenario that will happen?

What will help you keep calm and not get agitated when that happens?

Optional Exercise:

Record below if that trigger actually happened.

How did it feel to be prepared? Did it go well? If not, what could you have done better?

Additional thoughts...

I10: Model It

Each one of us will have had at least one role model, even as a child. It might have been a famous personality, your parent, teacher, just anyone you might have admired for some quality or skill they had.

My mother has been my role model from when I was a small girl. I used to spend a lot of time with my mom, as my dad was mostly out for work. She has taught me more about life than any book could have. She is a strong woman and has single-handedly overcome a lot of difficult situations. I have unknowingly taken up many positive traits from her, either by direct training or just by observing her.

Growing up, I did not have just one person as a role model. I derive inspiration from a lot of people I meet in my day-to-day life. I use all these learnings to empower and motivate myself.

Who did you want to model after as a CHILD?

Some questions I often receive on this exercise:

- Should it be only a role model from childhood?

For this task - yes, start with it. You can then add more to the mix—just make sure they positively influence you and share similar values.

- Why can I not start with someone I recently admire?
  For two reasons. 1) As grownups, we lose our innocence; we unknowingly have motives to like someone. 2) Why not go down your memory lane, acknowledge someone you like(d), and understand why?

MODEL IT

INTROSPECTION NO 10 DATE:

Whom did you want to emulate as a CHILD?

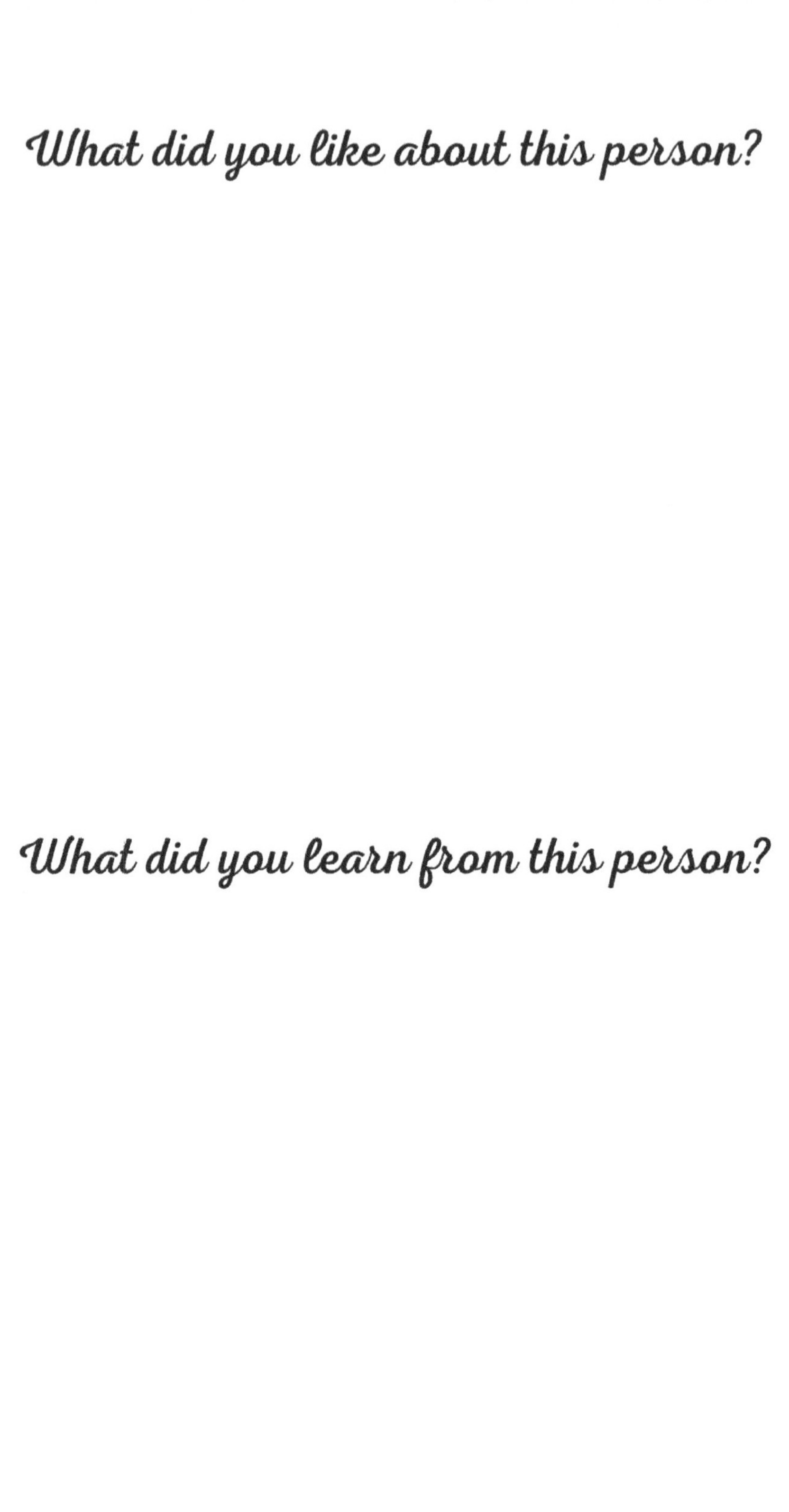
What did you like about this person?
What did you learn from this person?

Any skill or quality you have even the slightest resemblance with this person?

Is this person still your role model?

If not, why? Is it not relevant anymore?

111: E.A.T.

Wait, EAT? No, E.A.T., aka Expressive Art Therapy.

Art therapy is a proven technique to help people suffering from mental blocks or trauma. It is a potent healing strategy to empty one's inner state of mind and explore various parts of themselves—interests, conflicts, and such.

In this healing-centered exercise, you will express yourself without words, with an art form that you know. You can draw, paint or create a piece of craft like sculpture/jewelry; you may also choose to sew, compose music or just dance it out. Or you can do them all! You do not have to be an artist or someone very skilled with crafts. Express what resonates with you using any known art form and let your light shine through!

Once you are done, if you find art helped you express yourself better, trained art therapists can help you at a deeper level with a one-one connection. While choosing an art therapist, just ensure they are formally trained in visual art and psychology. Remember, not all of them help interpret your art; they may use various techniques. Have an open conversation about your needs before you commit to them.

Do not do this only as part of this exercise or when you are stressed. Incorporate this as part of your schedule; do it often, do it "just because," do it without reason. You will start finding it very therapeutic.

"Art washes from the soul the dust of everyday life." – Pablo Picasso.

E.A.T

INTROSPECTION NO 11 DATE:

Use this space, if needed, to express yourself through art

112: Do-Over or Let Go?

Every person must have done something wrong in their life, something they wish they had not done. Do you carry any regrets?

Mental stress comes by and large because of not letting go of your pain, regrets, and mistakes because we often live in the past. But from today, choose to live in the present. It might seem an uphill task and almost impossible to achieve. But you need to do it for your own well-being. You need to make a conscious choice to release anything that makes you unhappy or does not serve your life's purpose.

Letting go of hurt does not happen overnight. As with anything, it takes time and practice. Sometimes, you take some steps forward but fall two steps down. That is fine, as long as you strive to take the next step forward, albeit small.

Sometimes, very rarely though, life gives us another chance. You may have an opportunity to correct it. Let us call it the do-over. If you have even a sliver of hope that the do-over will improve your life, take that chance boldly. Do not fear. If you do not succeed, at least be happy that you tried. You can now come to terms with it.

So, what is it going to be? Do-over or let go?

DO-OVER OR LET-GO

INTROSPECTION NO 12 DATE:

If you had to mention the most regretful action in your life, what would it be? Why?

How did that mistake affect your life?

How differently could you have done it?

Did you learn anything from that mistake?

Now ... the crucial question set:

- *Do you still hold a chance to correct it?*
- *If corrected, will it positively impact your life and others dependent on you?*

Did you answer Yes & Yes? Marvelous! You chose the "DO-OVER." Gather the courage with all your might to right the wrong. Don't overthink and just do it!

If you have any other answer set - Just ... LET IT GO...

Release it naturally so that you can free your mind to think and act in the present. Your past does not define you. Do not hold on to it tightly. Remove that blockage from your heart—it is unnecessary baggage.

If you are not taking this action now, you might be in the same state years later. As long as you live in your tangled past, you will never be able to march forward and take charge of your life.

Seek answers and learn from your past experiences.

Have compassion for yourself in this liberating journey.

You are ready to move on!

END OF ZONE 1 - INTROSPECT

You have come to the end of Zone 1, INTROSPECT. How do you feel now?

If you need to re-do any particular exercise or all of them, you can. There is no fixed time to finish a zone. We are not in a race. Move to the next zone only if you feel you have emptied your mind at least 70% - 80%. It is crucial because a constipated mind will not be able to appreciate the beauty within and around.

If you have reached this section after completing all the exercises and are ready to move on to the next zone, I would have to really say, "Hats Off!" It will not have been an easy task to let your heart out. It takes immense courage to vent without any judgment and to identify/acknowledge your stressors. And you have done it, so give yourself credit. You cannot start healing if you do not know what is hurting you.

In the past, things may not have worked the way you planned, that is absolutely fine. But, at least you have come to terms with it.

Let go of your regrets! Forgive yourself! Move beyond them!

What did you get from reliving your past?

Determination? Resilience? Nice!

Just sad thoughts? Do not give up yet! Miracles do not play favorites. They happen to everyone, only when you start to believe. Do not be a skeptic! Truly believe that you are destined for more incredible things in life.

Love yourself just a tad more now. You are rediscovering yourself. You are taking magical steps to become happier and align with your vision.

CHECK-POINT

DATE:

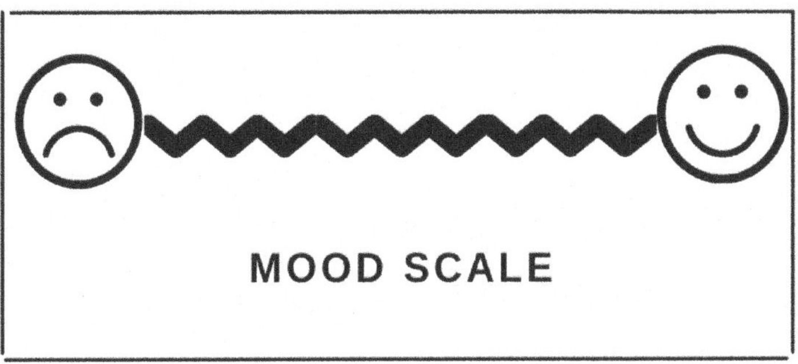

Add just a little note to record how you feel.

Has the scale gotten better from the last time you did this?

What has been a great accomplishment in the last two weeks?

ZONE 2 - CONNECT

The simple exercises in Zone 1 would have helped you open up your past, secrets, pain, mistakes, regrets, goals, and many other things about you. Zone 2, CONNECT, will help you channel your energy in the present.

It is okay if you do not have all the answers now. It is okay if you do not have it all under control.

Don't overthink. Don't judge. Don't complicate.

Inhale... Exhale... Relax... Reflect...

Everything is right where it has to be. Just believe...

Trust the process. Everything is happening for YOUR greater good.

Are you ready to release the past, connect better with the present and architect your future?

C1: Dear Diary...

All along this transformation journey, you may have felt a variety of emotions. Overall, you should definitely be feeling lighter than when you started. Think about all the happy moments as you connected with yourself. Pen them down in the journal area.

Once you are done reflecting, you need to record the next section, "My life as it will be." To answer this, think about what your vision is. What do you really want to achieve in this lifetime? Then answer the crux questions: What are your values? How do you want to structure your life going forward? What are your priorities? This will become your commandment. So, while you write all of this down, just focus on what YOU truly want.

You can write as much as you want. And you should.

Align your thoughts with your vision. Think about your morning routines, relationship with your spouse/kids/parents, the traits you need to change, how to face your workplace battles, your overall attitude towards life, how to treat yourself, any new habits to follow, etc. Write them all out.

Ready to build the life of your dreams?

DEAR DIARY

CONNECTION NO 1 DATE:

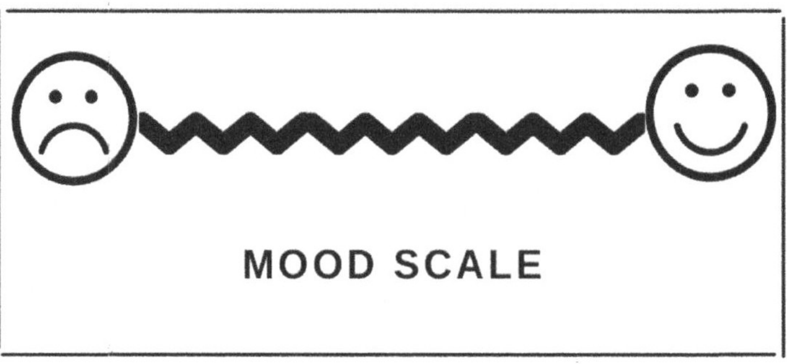

How are you feeling today?

What really made you happy in the last few weeks?

Learned anything new? Helped anyone random?

My life as it will be ..

C2: Blocked Out

How many friends do you have?

I am not talking about the 'connections' on your social media accounts. How many of them genuinely feel triumphant when you succeed and would be ready to lay down their lives to get you out of big trouble? Will you not be in contact with those friends, even if you are not connected on social media?

Sadly, these days, one's worth is determined by the number of friends/followers one has on social media. When I told one of my colleagues that I do not have any social media accounts, her reaction was, "Are you serious?" I was in touch with my family and friends before any of these existed and will continue to be. I am kind of old-school that way.

It is not that I am totally against it. It was just a lack of interest initially. I later realized that there has been a steep increase in unhealthy comparisons with the advent of social media. "They have gone on that vacation that we have always wanted to" or "How could they afford that big house?" or "How does she look so thin even after two kids?" and many more.

What you see on social media may/may not be the absolute truth. We know that people showcase the best aspects of their lives. Still, it is tough not to compare with our own life. It results in chaos in your mind, family life and whatnot!

Do you have connections on social media you haven't spoken to in a long time? Have you scrolled their pictures only to have a casual peek into their life? Well, they are posting it for us to see, right? Okay, you have seen. Now what?

Do you feel motivated and inspired to get better at your own life? No other comparisons at all? If YES, wow, I am impressed! You can move on to the next exercise. If NO, please continue to read.

If there was even an iota of jealousy or desperation, why do it?

Your key takeaway from this exercise is that you will block or unfollow your social media connections (again - not friends, just connections) who offer you nothing positive but only foster negativity within you. Do not do it all at once. Make a gradual transition. If someone's name pops out while you are reading this and you want to block that person, go ahead; maybe two next week and 10 in the next month.

Are you not convinced? That is fine. You may choose to skip this task. This is an optional exercise but highly recommended. However, promise yourself to reduce your time on mindless scrolling, not make any unhealthy comparisons and not have any self-esteem issues.

It is their life they are living. You know how to live yours and you will, GRANDEOUSLY!

Just give it the time!

C3: Dear Future Me

Human life is transient, no doubt. But wouldn't it be magical if you were to receive a message in your future from your past?

Yes, you will be the same person; maybe more mature, wiser, with a different perspective on life in general. It will be fun to read what your younger self had to say.

https://www.futureme.org/

Just head on to this website and write letters to yourself, to be delivered at a preferred date in the future as you like, say six months or one year or ten years. There is no cost involved with this. Your letter could be filled with advice, something to look out for, stop worrying about, or something silly (like "Please, please never get bangs!"). Even if it does not sound appealing to read about it now, do it anyway.

I have used this website a lot to write to my future self and always timed the letters to arrive on my birthday every year. It had a double benefit for me. Writing the letter had a cathartic effect in the first place. Besides, when I read it a year later, I felt emotional, pleasantly surprised, and always in tears of joy.

Are you not a website person? No problem. You can still write yourself a letter and put it away in some place that you don't frequently visit. Or if you have someone around, ask them to hide it in some spot. It may not have the same effect if you find it quickly or if someone else finds it out, but you can still try.

"Dear Me in 2030,

I know you are well. There are some things I think you really need to know..."

C4: Reflect Upon Self

Between dawns and dusks and dawns, life goes on.

We slog to achieve our goals. Or sometimes, we just slog without any goals. How many of us stop to smell the roses? Or at least smell something? How many of us self-reflect?

Today, you will give your inner critic something to think about. You are going to reflect upon yourself—on the good and the bad. This task will have some prompts to reflect on. It is just a start. Make it a routine.

Think about your goals, values, beliefs, what went wrong, what went right, anything and everything.

Self-reflection is a powerful tool to help you understand more about your true purpose in life. It helps put things in perspective. It enables you to assess if you are truly happy or need any tweaks to be done somewhere.

Reflect more. Reflect often.

You will learn and improvise. You will align.

REFLECT UPON SELF

CONNECTION NO 4 DATE:

When was the last time you spoke up for yourself? For what?

Did you trash any negative talk from others in the last year and believe in yourself?

It does not matter if you succeeded or not. How did it feel to believe?

When was the last time you were assertive?

Keep in mind -

'Saying NO' to things you are not comfortable with does not make you selfish.

It makes you more considerate of your feelings.

When was the last time you reacted positively to criticism?

What were you criticized for?

Refer to the goals you wrote down in Introspection 3.

How many of them have you achieved?

Pick one that is yet to be done.

List two things you will do this month to move closer towards that goal.

C5: Self-Care

Is Self-Care yet another item on your To-Do list?

Mine was!

As my day-to-day life got more exhausting and stressful, many self-help books I read suggested practicing self-care. So I did exactly what was asked of me every month. I went to the mall, had a spa day, ate loads of chocolates and ice creams, had my "me time," joined a Tai-Chi class, watched *Tom and Jerry* series (I always find them hilarious!) and many more.

I should have felt happy after that, right? Yes, maybe for the next 30 minutes or an hour.

Little did I know then that I was using self-care as a temporary escape route from the mundane life, only to return to my regular self. I was using it to numb the heaviness inside. It provided me temporary relief, and the pain always came back.

Self-Care is not a once-a-month ritual. You will have to be very consistent at it. You must do it multiple times a week, sometimes multiple times a day. You need to do it because it brings you joy, not because someone asked you to. YOU will have to find out what would give you abundant happiness. It could be meeting your friends every Friday for dinner, trekking on Saturday mornings, cooking for loved ones every once in a while, listening to your favorite music while driving to work, dressing up well and heading out, all of these and more. Do not force it; make it happen naturally.

Make it a way of life and thank me later!

SELF-CARE

CONNECTION NO 5 DATE:

What will bring you joy? What do you need to do to get that?

This is a living question; whenever something comes into your mind, keep updating this space & start incorporating it.

C6: What Is Your Worth?

What was your answer when you read the heading? Record it below.

The car you drive, your grades, your appearance, your job title, your savings—they do not measure your worth. In fact, there is no metric to measure your self-worth. It is just how highly you think of yourself. It is a somewhat abstract concept, albeit very important.

I have seen that people who feel very worthy are often very motivated and determined because they are connected to their core. They know precisely what and how to achieve because they feel they are worthy of it.

If you need a little motivation, here are a few ways to help you improve your self-worth. Trust me; I have done every single one of them, and they work!

- Avoid perfectionism. Often, people get frustrated with life because they are donning too many hats and trying to be the best version of themselves in everything. Perfection in every aspect of life is not achievable, and if you are trying to do that as I did, you will face burnout. It is okay to falter, completely okay!

- Discard your negative filter. Pondering over only the negatives in your life can make your life very pathetic. Stop entertaining any of these thoughts - *Why does this happen only to me?* or *What did I do to deserve all this?* or *God ... there are other people in the world to pull down, you know!* Start by countering your mind with something positive for every negative thought.

- Embrace yourself. Forgive yourselves for any mistakes you may have made previously. Drop the guilt! Accept the good, bad, and ugly—your flaws, fears, disabilities, and skills. It is okay if you cannot flaunt it, but that defines you. Be at peace with it!

- Never call yourself names. Calling yourself a name reduces you from a human to a single element of yourself that you do not like. You are not a “Total Failure” if you get fired from your job or “Hopeless” if your spouse just divorced you. You just faced a setback that you can rise from, stronger than ever!

- Listen to these two Brené Brown videos on YouTube. They really help.

  - Listening to shame -> https://www.youtube.com/watch?v=psN1DORYYV0
  - The power of vulnerability -> https://www.youtube.com/watch?v=iCvmsMzlF7o

C7: Let Go of Sadness

Do you have a broken heart? Or are you shielding yourself from heartbreak by faking joy? It doesn't work, does it?

Loss of a dear one, breakup, betrayal, rejection, and any heartbreak cause a feeling of emptiness. It feels as if all your joy has been sucked out with a straw. You may not be able to put words to it. You just feel it—a never-ending spiral of sadness.

I lost my dad to cancer. He refused to visit the doctors for initial symptoms, and when he did at my behest, the doctors made a wrong diagnosis. When it was finally found, it was too late.

I used to berate myself over and over that it happened because I was geographically so far away from him. I was the daughter he could not win an argument with. If I stayed close, I would not have taken "No" for an answer and would have taken him to the doctors much sooner. He could have lived longer.

Even after he passed, I did not handle it well. I would never talk about it. It took me so much reading, contemplation, realization and understanding to do away with the guilt first and grieve next.

No, it was not easy. But I have come to terms with it.

A lot of life's happenings do not have a reason. And that is the beauty of life. We simply do not know what we did to endure any pain. You cannot control them. Nor can you change the past. But you can learn to accept and try to move on. Yes, it will be challenging to start with. You may also experience feelings of guilt or shame. However, you will emerge stronger once you have dealt with it.

Here are few things I learned along the way:

- Be kind to yourself as you grieve. Do not set a time limit for when you should be done grieving. Do not let anyone set you a timer either.

- Distract yourself when the pain becomes unbearable. Start a new hobby; get a new pet; spend time with dear ones or in healthy solitude (not isolation).

- Choose activities you like and do them consistently - no limits:

- Physical Exertion: walk, bike, swim, trek/hike, do yoga, play sports, do gardening

- De-Clutter Your Space: organize, clean, decorate

- Hobbies: listen to music, cook, draw, play an instrument, write

- Personal Care: meditate, sleep well, eat healthily

- Socialize: call /text a friend, visit family, join a support group

- Other Diversions: shop, focus more at work, get a new haircut

Whatever has happened is a thing of the past, but find ways that help you feel like there is hope for your future.

Sending you hugs across the miles as you come to terms with sad events of your past.

Time will heal your wounds, and you will find happiness in other things.

You WILL heal!

END OF ZONE 2 - CONNECT

We have completed the zone 'Connect.' Here is a task before you read further:

END OF ZONE 2

DATE:

Draw a beautiful garden.

What does your garden have?

Let me guess - A lot of flowering plants and trees, a bench, a picket fence, fountain, maybe a rainbow in the sky?

Did it have any dead plants or trees? Why not? Because they take away the beauty of the garden. Correct?

When you care so much for an imaginary garden, how much more should you care for your mind and heart? Do they not deserve to be beautiful?

All negative emotions in the likes of anger, guilt, self-doubt, jealousy, and shame are the dead-weights in your life. In the previous exercises, you have been encouraged to remove many of these weeds that you were watering unknowingly.

You have started connecting with your true self. Remember, this is just the beginning. There may be a temporary setback as you continue your journey, but always remember that it is just a phase. You have all the resources you need to get yourself back on track. You will even learn new things along your way to help you with your endeavor.

Just be patient with yourself in the process. You got this!

ZONE 3 - EMPOWER

Honor yourself for getting to the stage you are at. It is hard work shedding all that negativity, and it takes a strong mind and heart.

You are now entering an exceptional zone.

Everything is coming together, finally. Just stay focused on your intentions with a never wavering trust. You will start manifesting abundant happiness.

Believe... Better things are coming... Better days are coming...

Direct your focus and energy towards your healing and see miracles unfold themselves right in front of your eyes.

The exercises in this zone will provide you a lot of nourishment, much-needed healing, and you will eventually find answers to your questions. The journey may be intimidating and scary at the start. Take some steps every day towards the goal. Rest if you need to, but do not quit.

Keep going!

CHECK-POINT

DATE:

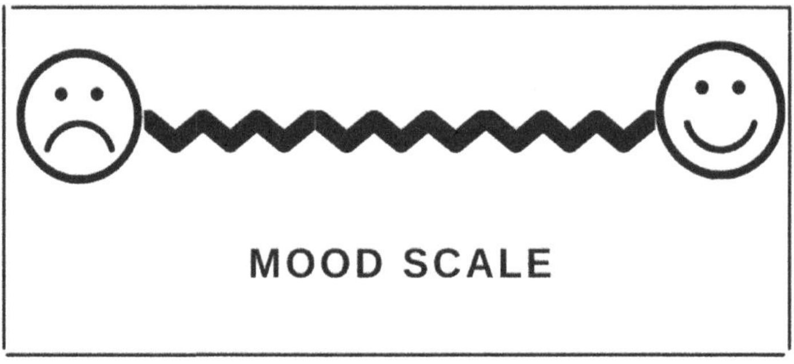

Add just a little note to record how you feel.

Has the scale gotten better from the last time you did this?

What has been a great accomplishment in the last two weeks?

E1: Gratitude

You will have heard this a lot or may have even bought a gratitude journal. Is it that important? And more importantly, why?

In today's busy world, it is easy to lose sight of what we are grateful for and what makes us happy. With a grateful heart, you become powerful; when you express it, you become unstoppable.

Why should the other person know that you are thankful for them? Imagine buying a gift, wrapping it beautifully with ribbons and bows, but not giving it to the intended person. It does not fulfill the purpose much, does it?

Make gratitude a habit! It helps you appreciate the small and big things in life. You start noticing the positives more and start looking for the silver lining even when the going gets tough.

In this world full of chaos, ground yourself with all the beautiful things going on in your life. It helps you develop a positive attitude towards life.

Do this more and make it a way of life!

GRATITUDE

EMPOWERMENT NO 1 DATE:

What is something that you have taken for granted all along, that you have never felt grateful for?

What is some material possession that you frequently use, did not have a year back, but you have now?

How does it make your life easier/better?

Which human being, living or dead, are you immeasurably grateful for? What did they teach you?

Who is the first person you would call if you needed to rant?

How does that make you feel to know that someone is there for you?

What is one mistake in life that taught you something significant?

How grateful are you for that lesson?

Anything else that you are grateful for?

Who are going to call right after this to say, "Thanks"?

E2: Bucket List

This is one of the most widely heard phrases in recent times. For those who don't know, a Bucket List is just a list of things you would like to do or experience before you reach a certain age (or while you are still alive). Is your mind screaming, *I know what I want to do, why list them out?*

Creating a bucket list by itself is very satisfying, and when you start crossing off one by one, it is very liberating. It gives you a feeling that you are living your life the way you want. Also, you can start tracking them, and they are not lost in the winds.

A few pointers to help you when you create your list:

- Each one of them has to be YOUR WISH.

- You do not have to ram your brain to bring out 50 things; you can list items as they strike you.

- It does not always have to be elaborate or trendy, like skydiving or an Alaskan cruise. It could be learning a new skill or eating at a favorite restaurant just by yourself.

- Make it a mix of short-term and long-term goals so that you will always find motivation.

- Do not focus only on just completing all of them. You will have to experience every one of them deeply.

If you need some ideas or motivation, head on to https://bucketlist.org/. Just a word of caution; if you do get some inspiration from elsewhere, make sure it aligns with your physical and mental strength before adding it to your mix.

MY BUCKET LIST

EMPOWERMENT NO 2 DATE:

My bucket list ---

E3: Set Healthy Boundaries

This is a very important topic.

What are personal boundaries? They are an invisible limit or marking space of what you will allow or not allow in your personal space. You can set boundaries at work, in family, with friends, with kids, and everywhere you deem fit. Healthy boundaries help you act according to your beliefs, likes, and values.

I have come across less than a handful of people who have effectively enforced healthy boundaries. People do not establish and enforce limits for fear of not being liked or being called selfish, or fear of hurting others' feelings. Some people do not even know their boundaries as they are so used to doing things other people demand.

Here are some quick tips to help mark your boundaries:

- Align your boundaries with your core values.

- Identify what makes you uncomfortable (this will relate back to your wants, likes, or beliefs).

- Have an open mind to list down who is manipulating you and why.

Once you have defined your boundaries, below are a few pointers that will help you communicate and enforce them successfully:

- Lose the Fear of Conflict. Everyone is different. You can have specific views about something that differ from all others in your gang. That is perfectly fine.

- Be assertive, not aggressive. Be respectful of the other person while reminding them of the boundary. Use phrases like, “I am not comfortable with...”, “I don't think that is the best option for me right now,” or simply, “I do not like this so much.”

- Do not feel the need to provide a lengthy explanation for why you cannot tolerate/accommodate something. It is your choice. The other person will have to deal with it, whether they like it or not.

- Do not fear, but be wary of the other person’s actions after your boundary has been communicated. If someone does not wish to continue to be your friend as you can no longer pay for their food daily, who is the loser? Was he/she even your friend to start with?

- Be aware of your environment or settings when you communicate. Think about things that could go wrong and be prepared. Put your safety above everything else and seek help if necessary.

- If the limits are violated continuously, make sure you communicate the consequences of their actions.

- Assess your boundaries from time to time and ensure they still fit in your scheme of things. Healthy boundaries are like a fence, not a brick wall. You can change them if you want to without compromising your overall beliefs or emotions.

If you were used to people walking all over you, they might not appreciate it when you start communicating your boundaries. You may receive a lot of criticism simply because they are threatened with losing something they were easily getting. And you may face resistance. Possible reactions may be, “You have changed,” or “What happened suddenly?” When these happen, simply repeat your boundary, and if need be, let them know why it is needed for you. Do not feel guilty because it is the right thing to do!

MY BOUNDARIES

EMPOWERMENT NO 3 DATE:

CORE VALUES

I AM OK WITH...
I AM NOT OK WITH...

I AM OK WITH...
I AM NOT OK WITH...

I AM OK WITH...
I AM NOT OK WITH...

E4: Energy Vampires

This topic is a continuation of the previous chapter, "Boundaries," but it is a bit different from the boundaries that we are typically used to. Most of the time, we do not even know such a thing exists.

Who/What are energy vampires? How do we identify them?

Have you come across any person who, knowingly or unknowingly, has a constant need to rant without caring for your time or space? Always focusing on every negative aspect of their lives? Always complaining and unappreciative? Not even willing to hear you talk? Do you feel very tired or emotionally down after most of their conversations? You can safely add such people to the list of your energy thieves.

I fell into such a trap myself and faced the wrath of not recognizing it early. This person used to be a good family friend and a former colleague. He had some problems at home and started visiting our home almost every day. His never-ending rants progressed to several hours in a day.

My husband and I used to feel sorry for him and tried our best to help him by hearing him out, offering help, good thoughts, prayers, etc. This went on for a good three months. We did not know he was stealing all our positivity. Bit by bit, negativity started looming in our lives.

While this went on, when I met him once at a work meeting, I casually mentioned that I was scared for my father's health as he was diagnosed with cancer. It was not even a rant; it was a two-minute talk. He did not let me finish and interrupted with, "Well, who does not have a problem in life?"

That is all! He did not want to hear more. I recognized his lack of interest and stopped abruptly. I had been watchful ever since. He did not check on my dad after but continued to ask for help here and there.

When I mentioned all my observations to my husband, he dismissed it as a rare occurrence. Later, when my husband had a similar conversation with this friend, his response was a xerox of what happened with me. My husband could not believe it. That is when the thought struck that he was just using us all along. We decided not to let this person even remotely into our lives any further. And we have been keeping up with it!

Another aspect of Energy Vampires is things/activities that drain your energy and those you have the slightest interest in doing. Since we have addressed many of these in earlier activities, let us continue focusing on the “people” type.

'Energy Vampires' may be anywhere—at work, in your social circle, family, or even your spouse. Identify them.

Some of them may be doing it unknowingly; you may educate them on why it is bad for you and them to linger in negativity. As a result, they may change for the better.

Some may not change, or they may do it knowingly as though you owe them this. My best advice would be to steer clear of such people, if possible, as they will successfully drain out all your energy and positivity. Sometimes, when you cannot avoid such people depending on how you are related to them, you will have to resort to setting boundaries. If you feel the need, you can listen to them without it impacting you. You are not required to provide any advice or solve any problems for them.

Protect your energy. Let it not be leeched!

E5: Meditate

Meditation is a powerful tool for better physical and mental health. You will probably have heard or read about its benefits a multitude of times. I, too, tried doing it. For a week. Then life came and it got sidelined. There were few things I started out wrong. Since I corrected them, meditation is now consistent in my routine.

There are different types of meditation, and there is no one-size-fits-all. You will have to find out what you need out of it and what works best for you.

Out of all the different techniques I have tried, I like Spiritual Meditation the best. I also practice Mantra Meditation, Mindfulness Meditation, and Pranayama. I try to mix them in my schedule. Next on my list is Transcendental Meditation.

Some pointers to have in mind for a better result with meditation:

- Try to meditate in the morning, before you face everything else in your day. If you have insomnia, you may do it before bedtime. It has been proven to help with it.

- Do it at the same time every day.

- Start small and then increase by increments. Begin with 10 minutes a day.

- Set up a space where you will meditate. That will be your Meditation Zone. Keep it clean, free of clutter.

- Put your distractions, such as the phone, out of the way for the duration of meditation.

- Meditating with some peaceful music may be helpful in the beginning. There are tons of meditation music videos online.

- Do not worry about the proper position or hand placement. Sit straight, very comfortably.

- Just breathe! Observe your breath with every deep Inhale/Exhale.

- Do not be hard on yourself if your mind wanders. If specific thoughts come to your mind during meditation, do not focus on driving them away. Do not get into the details. Instead, acknowledge them and move on.

- Do not expect miracles in a day or even a week. As with anything, you need to be ready to devote time and effort to start seeing results.

If you still find it difficult, you can use Guided Meditation Apps/join a local class. Here are my favorite apps: HeadSpace, Calm, Simple Habit.

Meditate... Recharge... Connect... Transcend...

E6: In Who/What You Trust

This is a very special chapter for me. What I am today and what I will be tomorrow is all due to Him!

Fear not! I am not here to advocate my spiritual beliefs. Not only will it sound ridiculous, but it is also disrespectful to you.

However, I would like to document something.

Spiritually integrated care is interlaced with mental health programs in many hospitals and clinics due to the overwhelming responses. Combining faith, nature, meditation, and mindfulness into the therapeutic process has proved to improve treatment plans and outcomes.

You do not have to believe in God. Even if you do, you do not have to follow a particular religion/practice a specific form of worship. You may call it The Universe or Nature or just Higher Power.

Or you may find it all meaningless. That is fine. But just know that as one maneuvers through the web of life and its events, it helps to believe and hold on to something beyond human understanding. Beyond science.

It helps you find purpose and life's meaning, helps you cope with stress in times of uncertainty, and most importantly, it instills hope for a better tomorrow.

Try it if you like; ignore it if you hate—that is your choice. But do not waver in your belief. Have clarity and go on! Nothing can or will stop you!

E7: Manifest What You Want

Do you believe in the Law of Attraction? Do you have a "Manifestation Board" yet?

Also called a "Vision Board" or "Intention Board," it is a powerful tool to keep your thoughts and actions aligned with your goals. They serve as a reminder of the small and big dreams for your future. Creating this is a healing process by itself, and it allows you to think deeply about what you want to manifest in your future.

It can be made both physically or electronically. I prefer the physical version as you can hang it in a place where you will see it frequently and thus be reminded of it multiple times a day.

If you prefer the online version instead, head on to http://www.gomoodboard.com/

What should you have on it? Anything that you want in your life, basically. Things that inspire you, your goals (personal/professional/health/relationship), dreams (not just materialistic ones), travel goals, quotes, pictures... Remember the bucket list you created earlier? Why don't you add something from there onto your board?

You can organize the goals by niche, or you can have them all bundled. You can even have a separate board for your personal and professional lives. I just have one board and update it half-yearly/on a need basis, removing those still not relevant and adding new ones. It does not have rigid rules. Let your creativity and individuality play!

Visualize these positive thoughts frequently and watch them turn into a reality. Continue to strive for each one of them. Let them not daunt you or scare you. Believe until they manifest; do not overthink how they will happen or when they will happen. Just strongly believe that you deserve every ounce of each. Because you do!

END OF ZONE 3 - EMPOWER

Have I felt that bad things chose only me in the entire world? Yes, until a few years back!

Did I bounce back from the deep rut? Yes!

I used to be very skeptical of the things people said about 'being positive' and such. They seemed fake and phony. And quite frankly, they did not work initially. Then I figured out the secret.

Until you process the negativity hidden even in the deepest corners of your mind and heart, whatever actions you do to stay positive will be futile. Legitimate feelings of stress, anxiety, or sadness need to be processed. You cannot mask them with optimistic phrases or by hearing pep talks. It is a process.

Having a positive outlook on life does not mean you have to stay positive even when the saddest of things happen. It means that even on hard days, you know that better ones are coming. It is completely okay to not be okay! Just do not get stuck in all the negativity.

You now have the tools and clarity to get uplifted even in the toughest of moments. All the chapters and exercises in this guided journal are stepping stones to get you tuned to feeling more empowered.

You can download a copy of the exercises you need to repeat from my website.
Link: http://rakwrites.com/the-resources
Password: H@ppyme123

Use them regularly. Make it a practice. Select one exercise. Or re-do the entire set. Every time you complete this journey, you will discover a new version of yourself.

I hope this book has helped you on some level. As an emerging author, your review will help spread the word about this book and empower more lives.

As you go through the process of implementing these techniques and start living the life of your dreams, connect with me to ask a question or provide a constructive feedback, or join the private group to connect and tell your story.

https://www.facebook.com/groups/introspectconnectempower

https://www.instagram.com/rakwrites/

BE HAPPY, BE POSITIVE, BE YOU!

Here is a tight virtual hug with tons of love and wishes for choosing YOU!

CHEERS ~

Made in the USA
Coppell, TX
27 July 2021